Scamp

Story by Jan Weeks

Illustrated by Elise Hurst

PM Plus Chapter Books
Emerald

U.S. Edition © 2006 Harcourt Achieve Inc.
10801 N. MoPac Expressway
Building #3
Austin, TX 78759
www.harcourtachieve.com

Text © 2003 Cengage Learning Australia Pty Limited
Illustrations © 2003 Cengage Learning Australia Pty Limited
Originally published in Australia by Cengage Learning Australia

7 8 9 10 11 12   1957   14 13 12 11
4500334306

Text: Jan Weeks
Illustrations: Elise Hurst
Printed in China by 1010 Printing International Ltd

Scamp
ISBN 978 0 75 784119 4

Contents

CHAPTER ONE
Tilly

Summer vacation is my favorite time of the year. My family and I go to our cottage at Mermaid Point on the coast. Our cottage sits high on a hill and faces the ocean.

I like Mermaid Point a lot. I go for walks along the beach and feel the salt spray on my face. At night, I listen to the waves crash against the rocks. I can't see any of Mermaid Point because I'm visually impaired. I only see shadows.

Dad tells me when he sees dolphins swimming in the ocean. One day, a fisherman caught a big fish. "It's a beauty!" I heard him cry out. Then he held it for me so that I could feel its scales. They felt really slimy! Dad said they were very shiny, too.

Our cottage has two floors. We live upstairs. I easily manage the stairs because they have a wooden rail, and I know exactly where to find the steps.

Behind our cottage is a small forest full of wildlife. One night, a couple of years ago, Mom saw an opossum high in the trees. She prepared a dish of ripe fruit and crunchy vegetables and gave it to me.

"Put the dish on the balcony, Dylan," she said. "That opossum might like some!"

She was right! Every night after that, the opossum came back, waiting for food. I soon felt like she was my pet, and so I named her Tilly.

"That opossum seems to know the minute we arrive!" Mom said to me the last time we were back at the cottage. "It's as though she has a sixth sense."

Mom was right. Within minutes of arriving, Tilly climbed down the trees and onto our balcony. I heard the crackling of leaves and knew that Tilly was close by. She scampered along the top of the railing, and headed toward her dish.

"You feed her too much, Dylan!" Dad told me. "She's going to end up the size of a jumbo jet."

Tilly didn't seem to mind how much I fed her. She stayed at her dish, munching away, until she had eaten every last mouthful. Then she waited to see if I had anything else for her to eat!

Tilly wasn't afraid of me. She let me sit close to her while she ate. I think she knew that I would never hurt her.

I was glad Tilly trusted me. "You're my special friend, Tilly," I told her, softly.

CHAPTER TWO

Uncle Ray and Scamp

Tilly is scared of dogs. Mom says that if she hears one, she stands perfectly still, and waits for it to go away.

Sometimes Dad sees dead opossums in the woods. "If dogs are let out of their yards, they sometimes kill wildlife," he tells me.

I never used to like dogs either.

You see, a long time ago, a big dog knocked me down. I was walking and it ran right into me. I also thought all dogs were smelly and had fleas!

Mom, Dad, and my teacher at school used to tell me I could have a guide dog when I got older. Guide dogs are either german shepherds, labradors, or golden retrievers. They are specially trained to help people who can't see. But I didn't think I wanted one.

"They become like your eyes," my teacher once told me. "When you have a guide dog, you are more independent and are better able to take care of yourself."

My teacher didn't make me change my mind. I still didn't want a dog.

★ ★ ★

Usually, Tilly visited me by herself. But sometimes, she came with another opossum that we call Elephant. We call him Elephant because he sounds like one when he walks across our roof!

Elephant wasn't as shy as Tilly. Once, when Uncle Ray stayed with us, Elephant climbed onto Uncle Ray's shoulder! Boy, did that scare Uncle Ray. I heard him give a big yell!

Before our last vacation, Uncle Ray called Dad and asked if he could come to our cottage when we were there. He had a couple of weeks to spare before he went overseas to work and wanted to spend the time with us.

Dad was really pleased, but I wasn't.

I love Uncle Ray a lot. It's just that I didn't want Uncle Ray to bring his dog, Scamp. Scamp had belonged to my Aunt Pat before she died.

"Of course you can bring Scamp," I had heard Dad say to Uncle Ray, over the phone.

"Why did you tell Uncle Ray he could bring Scamp?" I asked Dad, later. "What about Tilly? She doesn't like dogs."

"Scamp will sleep in the house at night," Dad answered. "That way, he won't go anywhere near Tilly."

I hoped Dad was right.

CHAPTER THREE

Scamp Escapes!

Scamp wouldn't leave me alone! Every time I sat down, he tried to lick my hand or put his head in my lap, and expected me to pet him.

Whenever I went into the backyard, he was there, trying to get me to play with him.

"Go away!" I said and pushed Scamp away. "I don't like dogs!"

Mom tried to get me to feed Scamp, but I didn't want anything to do with him.

"He's really a friendly dog," Mom said. "If you give him a chance, you might even get to like him!"

I didn't want to like him.

★　★　★

One night, Scamp escaped out of the house. Someone had forgotten to latch the screen door that led to the balcony. I heard Scamp out on the balcony, barking.

I panicked – Tilly was eating her dinner. But she also heard the danger, and I heard her scampering off.

"Now look what you've done!" I yelled at whoever it was who had left the door open. "The dog's out!"

I was so upset that I tripped over a chair in the living room.

"There's no need for you to panic," Dad said, helping me to my feet. "Tilly's all right. I can hear her on the roof."

Scamp continued barking. I heard him run down the stairs, through the backyard, and into the woods.

Uncle Ray had rushed out the screen door, onto the balcony, as soon as Scamp had escaped. I heard him calling Scamp's name, trying to get him to come back. But Scamp was gone.

"I hope he doesn't hurt Tilly!" I said, loudly.

Eventually, Scamp came home. I was in bed, but I heard Uncle Ray softly open the balcony screen door and let Scamp in. Now I disliked Scamp even more than before.

The next night, I put out lots of Tilly's favorite fruit. I even asked Mom to chop it up into little pieces in the hope that Tilly would smell it.

"Tilly!" I called.

But Tilly didn't come for her dinner.

Eventually, Dad shone a flashlight into the trees but there were no opossums hiding in the branches.

"I hope Scamp hasn't hurt her," I said. I felt sick with worry.

CHAPTER FOUR
An Unlikely Hero

The next day, Dad's friend, Stephen, stopped in to see him. His cottage also backs up to the forest.

"That dog of yours is a hero," Stephen said to Uncle Ray.

I wondered what he meant. How could a dog that scared opossums be a hero?

"Didn't you hear the fox?" Stephen asked. "It tried to break into our rabbit hutch. If it hadn't been for your dog, the fox would have killed our rabbits."

So that explained why Scamp had been barking. He had heard the fox and had run out to scare it away. But I was still really angry, and I still didn't want to like Scamp.

★   ★   ★

It was really lonely at the cottage without Tilly. I missed her company. "I wish she'd come back," I said to Mom. "I really miss her."

But Tilly didn't come back. And neither did Elephant. The only animal I had around me was Scamp.

I stood in the backyard and felt Scamp push something wet into my hand. It was his ball.

"If you throw it, Scamp will bring it back to you," said Uncle Ray, gently.

I took the ball from Scamp's mouth and threw it as hard as I could, across the yard. I heard Scamp race through the dead leaves as he chased after it.

Then I heard Scamp run back to me, and I felt the wet ball being pushed back into my hand. Scamp panted as he waited for me to throw it again.

"Good dog!" I said without thinking.

The next morning, as I ate my breakfast, Uncle Ray asked me if I wanted to take Scamp for a walk.

I wondered how he thought I could do it.

"All you need to do is hold onto his leash," Uncle Ray said. "I'll come with you if you like. We'll go to the store. I want to buy a newspaper."

We went downstairs. I waited for Uncle Ray to put the leash on Scamp but, instead, he gave the leash to me.

"You can do it, Dylan," Uncle Ray told me, and put my hand on Scamp's collar. "You can feel where the leash clips onto his collar."

I was worried that Scamp would try to run away, but he didn't. He walked beside me all the way to the store.

"Your Aunt Pat used to take Scamp for lots of walks," Uncle Ray said. "They were always together. After she died, Scamp missed her for a long time. It's good that he's been able to make friends with you."

That night, Scamp put his furry head in my lap, and I didn't push him away.

CHAPTER FIVE

Old and New Friends

Not long after that, Uncle Ray had to leave. He had to go to catch his plane.

Before he left, Uncle Ray asked me if I wanted to look after Scamp while he was away. He said it would be for a long time.

Mom and Dad left the decision to me. They knew how I felt about dogs. But I wasn't sure how I felt. I *used* to be frightened of dogs, but Scamp had changed my feelings.

I still missed Tilly, but without Scamp I knew I would be really lonely.

"Of course I'll take care of him," I said as I patted Scamp. I was surprised at how happy I felt.

★ ★ ★

Scamp and I had to wait until the next break before we went back to the cottage. When we did, I was in for a wonderful surprise.

I was sitting inside the house with Scamp when I heard a noise. It was coming from the balcony.

At first, I thought it was Mom and Dad, but then they called out to me.

"There's someone out here who wants to see you!" they said.

I hurried out the screen door. Scamp didn't get up and follow me. He let me go by myself.

Once outside, I could barely believe what Mom told me.

"Tilly is back!" said Mom. I could tell from her voice she was smiling. "And she's brought a baby opossum with her!"

"That explains why we haven't seen her," Dad said. "Tilly's been very busy becoming a mother."

"What does the baby look like?" I asked, feeling really excited. "Is it just like Tilly?"

"What we can see of it!" Dad answered.

"The baby is clinging to Tilly's back. Tilly's fur hides some of it, but Tilly seems very proud," Mom said and we all laughed.

Tilly never visited me after that. That was the last time. I think she came back to let me know she was safe and that she'd had a baby. Now, whenever I think of Tilly and Elephant, I think of them in the woods, high up in a tree, taking care of their family.

And I know that they are happy because that's what opossums are meant to do. Dad says you can't keep wild animals as pets. They need to be free.

And that's true. But some animals are really great pets – especially Scamp.